9 Lessons
I Have Learned From

Fr. Felino

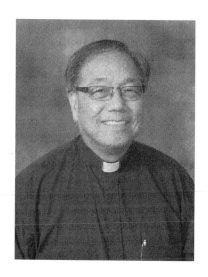

by

Fr. Vu Tran

Contents

Introduction...5

Lesson I..7

Lesson II...11

Lesson III..13

Lesson IV..15

Lesson V...19

Lesson VI..25

Lesson VII...27

Lesson VIII..29

Lesson IX..31

Closing..33

Happy Birthday

Fr. Felino

Introduction

After a decade of priesthood ministry in parish life, with much discernment, I decided that I needed to step back.

I recalled a story about St. Francis of Assisi. At the turning point in his life, Francis took off his all his garments in the public square in his home town. For me, this kind of shedding is a moment of complete transparency.

Many of us probably have things that we hide from God and from one another; These private secrets we hold on to that no one knows. I wonder why we hold on to them? Is it because we feel ashamed and embarrassed especially if it becomes public knowledge? Is it because we are worried that our reputation will be completely ruined once people know them? Would our life, our relationships, our career be in total jeopardy as soon as people find out? Is vulnerability a weakness and we should hide them and not wear them on our sleeves for everyone to know?

So, after much prayer and discernment, I asked the Archbishop for a time of rest and sabbatical. I needed more time for prayer, and honest evaluation of my spiritual status, prayer life, and physical well being.

After the sabbatical and retreats, which was a complete blessing, I was assigned by the Archbishop of Seattle and the Priest Placement Board to a parish cluster in South Seattle. The four cluster parishes are: St. Edward, St. George, St. Peter and St. Paul.

During this time, I assisted Fr. Felino who was the Pastor of these four parishes.

Admittedly, Fr. Felino, being fully human, is not perfect and has his imperfections. We all do! These imperfections can bring out the humanity within each of us.

But he also has many unique gifts and talents. His vision, personality, character, genuineness, honesty; some of these factors and many more, I truly admired.

In this short book, I want to share with you some of the valuable lessons for ministry that I learned from Fr. Felino. Here are the 9 lessons that I learned from him. Originally, the title of this book was 10 lessons I learned from Fr. Felino. But I couldn't think of a tenth lessons, so the title had to be slightly modified.

I think the experience of working with him has helped me to be a better priest. I think that it has help me become a better person. I think he will also help me be more effective in parish ministry in the future.

Lesson I

Refrain from saying "NO".

This is one of the first valuable lessons I learned from Fr. Felino. It is to try and refrain from saying "NO." Try not to use the word "NO".

Often times, parishioners approach the priest, pastoral ministers, or committee leaders, and make their requests. Some are good requests, others not so good.

For instance: "Father, could we use the church this evening for a gathering to pray and study the bible?"

I remembered a woman once approached me with a request. She said: "Many of our young families have gotten together. We want to cook for you. Is that OK? It seems that you're getting thin, and we want to make sure that our parish priest is well taken care of. We want to make sure that we are taking good care of you."

I quickly responded: "Well, I don't usually eat at home, because I'm trying to do more home visits. I like to visit parishioners at their homes. Also, parishioners sometimes invite me out to eat. If I have too much food in the refrigerator, I may not eat it, and it will probably be going to waste. Also, I'm trying to cut back on carbs. I'm trying to lose weight. So, I rather not."

When we are quick to say "NO" to someone's requests, suggestions or ideas, it can discourage them from approaching us in the future. It can also discourage them from wanting to serve.

If I put myself in the shoes of the parishioners, I learned that these requests, suggestions or ideas are not something that they take lightly. It's not something that they came up with, perhaps without deep reflection and consideration. They have may spent much time mulling it over. Moreover, it may have been the Holy Spirit who guided them in that direction.

When we quickly shut people down by quickly saying "NO", essentially we are implying: "Don't listen to the guidance of the Holy Spirit."

Instead, we want to encourage people to listen to God. It may be God who is actually speaking with them. We are here to help them discern whether or not the voices and inspirations are from God.

By saying "NO" too quickly, it may make them feel discouraged. It may make them reluctant to serve. They may think to themselves:

I never have any good ideas. Father doesn't want me to serve.

Try to associate the word "NO" with a red flag. Every time you use the word "NO", there should be a loud alarm going off in your head. If you accidentally use the word "NO" because of habit, just follow up with the words "I'm sorry."

Sometimes, people's ideas or suggestions are genuine. But the proposals may appear ridiculous, crazy or unreasonable.

Even during these crucial moments, it's important to be cautious and careful that we still don't use the word "NO."

Instead, we want to help them see the bigger picture. Perhaps, we may want to ask them: "Well, what do you think about this or that?" "What about this idea or that idea?" By using a different response method, you could avoid saying "NO", and also lead them towards a different pastoral direction, and still help them develop a willing spirit of service.

Try not to use the word "NO" when others approach you with a request.

Lesson II

Ministry of Presence

In these four parishes, there are so many different parish events and gatherings. Many times, it feels overwhelming. Imagine being a Pastor of four parishes and three schools.

Sometimes, the gatherings conflict with one another. Nevertheless, it's important that the priest is present at all of these gatherings.

Even if it's just for 5-10 minutes, just enough to say hello, give a little talk, thank the people, encourage the parishioners, and say a little prayer. The Ministry of Presence is vital and important to boost morale in the parish.

Whenever Fr. Felino is invited, he will most likely be there for a few minutes to an hour or two. Parishioners will totally understand that there is a conflict. They understand that he needs to get back on the road to another parish function. They will be grateful that he has taken the time in his busy schedule to be present.

I'm more of a private person, so most likely, I will pick and choose which functions I want to be present. This may not be the best practice.

People may feel neglected if the priest doesn't show up for the gathering.

I also learned to be ready at every gathering. Why? Because most likely, the priest will be asked to give a quick speech and say a quick prayer and blessing.

Normally, thanking the people for their generosity and wishing them God's blessings and graces is always a good idea, and follow up by a prayer thanking God for His providence through the work of human hands, and may the food which we are about to receive sustain us for the spiritual work at present and in the future.

The Ministry of Presence is a priceless pearl in the parish ministry.

Lesson III

Be Humble of Speech.

The third lesson that I learned from Fr. Felino is humility in speech. Perhaps, this is a common trait that is taught and practiced by many Filipinos.

I remembered one time at a Funeral, a son gave the Eulogy for his father. He shared that his father taught him to always be humble in speech. His father taught him a valuable lesson that he should never try to sound smarter than the other person, or speak with a condescending tone, or give people the impression that you are more intelligent or brighter than them, and yes, even if all of that may be true.

Try to be more silent and refrain from jumping too quickly to conclusions. It is so that we can practice listening to people and try to hear what they are actually saying.

Sometimes, people don't want you to do anything for them. Sometimes, they just don't want any of your advice. They may just want someone to listen. When we are too quick to speak, it may keep them from sharing. They may think to themselves: "I don't have good insights or ideas to share. I'll just keep my mouth shut."

Also, I learned this important lesson when I celebrated Mass with students and worked with the Confirmation students.

It dawned on me that sometimes when I ask questions, and students get it wrong, I would proceed to ask the same question to another student. I suddenly realized that the person may feel stupid or awful because they don't know the answer, or that they are afraid to take the risk, or because they are shy, etc. When a student takes a risk and raises their hand in the attempt to answer or share an insight, but doesn't answer a question correctly, and if I move on to another, the student may feel like a failure.

So I learned that it's important to stay with them. In other words, avoid looking at other hands that are being raised. Just stick with that particular one for the time being. Give that particular student another chance to answer. Give them another try to get it right. Give them another opportunity. It will encourage them to persevere. We could also give them some suggestions or assistance. Maybe even whisper the right answer to them. It's much better than just moving on to another person without giving them a second chance or a third try.

Be Humble of Speech

Lesson IV

Invite and Never Force

The fourth lesson I learn from Fr. Felino is to always invite people rather than forcing people to do something.

He would often invite me to Deanery Meetings, Council Meetings, and other gatherings. I usually don't like to attend meetings, so I politely turn it down. But it doesn't mean that he stops the invitations.

Whenever we have a parish function, gathering or an event, it's important to invite people. But at the same time, we must do so with respect to their freedom. Forcing people to do something takes their away their freedom, and disrespects their dignity.

If they happen to turn down the invitation, don't be quick to show disappointment or disapproval. Perhaps, it's not the right time. Maybe they're not spiritually or emotionally ready.

It doesn't mean not to invite them anymore because of their refusals. It's wise to persevere and keep consistent with the invitations despite the number of times they turn it down. By having a hopeful and positive attitude can make a difference in parish life.

In counseling couples who have difficulty in their relationship, I've learned that couples may have the best intentions, but their insistence may come across as applying pressure or force on the other. When this occurs, they may be infringing on the other person's freedom and choice.

For instance, if the woman wants to pursue a career of her own but her husband wants her to stay at home. Or if the husband forbids his wife to spend time with her friends for a book club or a gathering with her friends for a wine party.

Couples who learn to respect the freedom of the other, their relationship tends to work out better. I often hear about couples who, after their breakup, remain the best of friends. The irony is that, after their breakup, they feel closer to one another. They're no longer walking on egg shells. They can freely share what is on their mind without worrying too much about how it offends the other person.

A good advice may be for couples is to share their opinions, advices and suggestions with the other, but still respect the person's decision.

For instance: "Sweetheart, I don't think it's a good idea, but I will support you and your decisions." Or another example: "Honey, I think you are making a huge mistake. Here are the pros and cons of this decision. But if you feel that this is the right thing to do, please know that I will be by your side no matter what. You still have my support."

Sometimes, I would approach Fr. Felino with a request or a suggestion. Often, he takes the time to listen. He will encourage me to do what I think God wants me to do. For instance, I approached him about the possibility of learning Spanish, and being able to celebrate the Mass in Spanish. He was very much open to that idea.

Some of my good ideas, however, turn out not to be so good. Still, he does his best to listen and shows encouragement and support. He is not reluctant to disagree or share the reasons for his way of thinking. But in the end, he remains optimistic and positive.

Once, I remember attending a proposal within the Archdiocese about a program to improve our church. After attending it, I shared my negative thoughts with Fr. Felino. I told him that I don't think it will work out. This program was similar to many others that we have tried in the Archdiocese.

Despite the negative feedback, he still remained positive and optimistic. He shared that we have to at least give it a try. The positive and optimistic attitude is a sign of a good leader.

Once, I remember looking at the parish bulletin and noticing that our collections have been way down, and that our debt is still way over our head, and it wasn't getting any better. I asked him about his thoughts, and he simply said: "It could be much worse." For me, in that response, he embodies the virtue of hope.

Lesson V

Relying upon the Holy Spirit

In one of our Confirmation class, Fr. Felino was the guest speaker. He shared his insights about prayer. He shared about his experience with Lectio Divina, which means Divine Reading.

The Lectio Divina method allows us to reflect upon any passage in the Sacred Scriptures, and put ourselves into the story. By doing so, the story is not just something about the past. It actually comes to life.

There are four steps to Lectio Divina: Read, Meditate, Pray and Contemplate. The general idea is that by going through each word and biblical verse carefully and conscientiously, the Word of God is real and comes to life.

Because of my ten years of priesthood and eight years of seminary training, I'm familiar with many of the Scripture passages. I've heard them countless of times. I could recite many biblical verses by heart.

In many passages, I'm familiar with the Jewish background and traditions, the understanding of God based on certain passages, the theological implications and doctrinal truths formed from the passages.

For this particular class, Fr. Felino printed out the passage from the Gospel according to St. Luke 19:1-10. It was about the encounter of Jesus with Zacchaeus.

Certainly, I'm familiar with this passage about Zacchaeus, who was the chief tax-collector, and the one who climbed the sycamore tree to see Jesus because he was short in stature. I couldn't possibly learn anything new from his sharing.

But I learned a valuable lesson in that Confirmation class. I learned that before we use the four methods of Lectio Divine (read, meditate, pray and contemplate), we have to pray to the Holy Spirit. We need to ask for the Holy Spirit's guidance. So we spent some time saying the prayer to the Holy Spirit.

Here is the prayer to the Holy Spirit:

Come, Holy Spirit, fill the hearts of Thy faithful and enkindle in them the fire of Thy love. Send forth Thy Spirit and they shall be created. And Thou shalt renew the face of the earth. Let us pray. O God, Who didst instruct the hearts of the faithful by the light of the Holy Spirit, grant us in the same Spirit to be truly wise, and ever to rejoice in His consolation. Through Christ our Lord. Amen.

Amazingly, after the prayer to the Holy Spirit, I was able to see Jesus vividly.

The passage about Zacchaeus, for me, became a passage not just for a class assignment. It was a passage not just to be used as a reference for a scholarly examination. The passage was not just to be used for homilies and reflections.

It was not just a passage for the sake of evangelization and converting non-believers. It was not just a passage to use for sharing the faith with others. The passage was not just to learn and be familiar with the history and background of the story.

Amazingly, because of the Holy Spirit, I was able to see Jesus vividly. I could see Jesus standing right before me speaking with Zacchaeus.

I have to honestly admit, it was the strangest experience. And it felt wonderful!

It's kind of like the Holy Spirit gave me a different set of eyes. So that I could see Jesus clearly.

Thundercats

One of my favorite cartoons as a child was Thundercats, the original series (yes, I'm showing my age). My brothers and I never missed an episode. It was our favorite past time after school. Besides the Catholic Church, Thundercats was our religion.

In Thundercats, Lion-O, Lord of the Thundercats, had a special sword called the Sword of Omens. The sword is special because it emits a black and red Cat Signal to all the other Thundercats when Lion-O was in trouble.

But Lion-O had to use a formula to make the sword work. He would say: "Thunder, Thunder, Thunder, Thundercats, HO........" The signal shot towards the sky (kind of like the Batman signal), and all the other Thundercats could see it. Upon seeing the signal, they ran to help him defeat the evil lord (a mummy) called Mum-Ra.

The Sword of Omens also helped Lion-O when he is stuck, or doesn't understand something that is happening to the Thundercats.

Besides asking help from his ghost-mentor, Jaga (this would be like prayer to God), he would ask the Sword of Omens for help. But Lion-O did it in a peculiar way. He would raise the sword to his eyes (the handle part) and look through it. Then he would summon the sword with a formula: "Sword of Omens, give me sight, beyond sight."

By looking through the eyes of of the Sword of Omens, he could see other Thundercats who are in trouble. He could also see the present danger that the Thundercats were facing. He could also gain insight to solve difficult problems.

In a similar way, merely as an analogy, I think that the Holy Spirit is liken to the Sword of Omens. The Holy Spirit can give us sight beyond sight. The Holy Spirit can help us see Jesus vividly. When we read a particular passage from Sacred Scriptures, and don't understand its meaning, we can call upon the Holy Spirit for help and assistance.

The Holy Spirit will give us a different set of lens to see through. He will allow us to see into the mystery. He will help us to see Jesus and encounter him. That is what happened to me on the day that Fr. Felino gave the talk on Lectio Divina.

Nowadays, if I'm meditating on the Scriptures, or preparing for a homily, I will immediately ask the Holy Spirit for guidance and help. "Holy Spirit, help me to see Jesus. Speak to us what you want us to hear." I rarely did this in the past.

It's amazing that with the assistance from the Holy Spirit, it changes my attitude, my perception and my view towards scriptures.

Even more amazing is that the Holy Spirit will communicate to people what the Spirit wants them to hear. With the Holy Spirit, there is less effort, but with greater effectiveness.

Holy Spirit, help us to see Jesus vividly.

Lesson VI

Self-Discipline

One of the things that I admire about Fr. Felino is his self-discipline.

My bedroom is next to the stairs. So I could hear him walking up and down the stairs. He wakes up each day around 5:30 am for breakfast. He also sleeps early, around 10:30-11:00pm.

I'm the complete opposite. I'm a night owl. I usually stay up to 2am or 3am, watching television, surfing the internet, writing or reading. It's no surprise that sometimes I'll wake up late for prayer or Mass. Morning prayer is 7:30am. Mass is around 8:15am.

Because of my inconsistency, my internal clock is often screwed up. Sometimes on Mondays, I have to catch up on my sleep, by sleeping in until noontime.

With his strict discipline and routine, he could easily outlast me.

Self-Discipline also helps him deal with the emotional, roller-coaster factor. He prays, whether he feels like it or not.

As for me, I may only pray when I'm in a good mood. Being disciplined, however, can help establish a strong foundation in regards to the prayer life. If prayer is dependent upon emotions or mood, it may become irregular, and the danger is falling out of the habit of praying.

Many of us are familiar with the children's story about the Hare and Tortoise. The Tortoise won the race and beats the hare because of his discipline and consistency. This is a good lesson in self-discipline: "Slow and Steady wins the race."

Lesson VII

Living in Community

Another valuable lesson I learned from Fr. Felino is his preference to live in community. Some priests prefer to live in community while others prefer to live on their own. Some enjoy having others around while some like to have their own private space. Some are extraverts while others are introverts.

Fr. Felino doesn't mind having other priests stay at the Rectory. He actually enjoys the company of his fellow priests.

Currently, we have four priests living in one Rectory. So we learn to share the living space. We learn to share the kitchen. We learn to share what is in the refrigerator, and should not be surprised if something disappears the following day.

By living in community, we learn to get along. We learn to live together in a communal environment. We learn to tolerate differences. Someone once said: "It takes a Saint to live in community."

Also, three times a week, the priests get together for supper after evening prayer. It's a good time for us to share stories and listen to one another. We have a wonderful time, sharing things about our ministry, keeping each other updated about the latest news, sharing what we will be preaching on for the upcoming weekend, or help each by giving advice and insights.

Sometimes, we talk about our flock and discern better ways to assist them on the faith journey.

The meals are often enjoyable. We learn so much from each other's experience. And sometimes we poke fun of one another to keep each other humble. But it's all done in good fun.

Fr. Felino is also quick on his feet. He's a fast thinker. He doesn't let anything past him.

There are pros and cons about living in community. But there are valuable lessons to be learned when living in community.

Lesson VIII

Humor and Lightheartedness

One of the things I learn from Fr. Felino is that he has a good sense of humor because he tries to keep things light.

He has tons of funny stories, ready to share with anyone who would lend an ear. He always begins his homilies with a joke or some humor. Parishioners have shared that Fr. Felino often includes a joke or a humorous story in his homilies, retreats, talks and reflections. He enjoys seeing people laugh.

He also hands out prayer cards for people who answers questions correctly. He will do things to keep it lighthearted.

I seldom tell funny stories because normally it is not met with any laughter. I sometimes notice that people feel sorry for me afterwards.

We always have a wonderful time at the dinner table, with him sharing funny stories and antidotes. Ministry can sometimes be heavy. Even the Lord Jesus spoke about this: "Come to me, all you who labor and burdened, and I will give you rest. Take my yoke upon you and learn from me. My yoke is easy and my burden is light." "Come away and rest for yourselves awhile."

Once he shared a story about a married couple. The wife kept telling her husband that she has been having these strange dreams. She dreamed that on Valentine's Day, she will receive an expensive diamond necklace, ring and bracelet. She asked her husband for help in regards to the dream. The husband says to her: "Honey, you will understand on Valentine's Day." So, on Valentine's Day, the husband gives her gift. She unwraps the gift to find a book. The book is entitled: "The meaning of Dreams."

It is easy to allow the heaviness to creep in and take over our lives. It's more difficult to be lighthearted, but it's worth it in parish ministry.

Lesson IX

Total Dedication and Commitment

Fr. Felino once shared with me that he went to High School Seminary. He may have started the priesthood even younger.

For me, I started the Seminary when I went to college. Other priests have shared that they started the Seminary process much later in life. One person shared that he felt called to the priesthood just before he was about to get married. It's interesting how God calls people to ministry at different points in their life.

I once asked Fr. Felino if he ever thought about doing something different. He said he thought about it, but it didn't stick. He believed that God truly called him to the priesthood.

Fr. Felino has been a priest for a long time. He will be celebrating his 39 years of priesthood. It's not just the number of years of serving Christ. It's about the daily commitment of serving the Lord.

There's not a day that goes by that he's not thinking about the church. He probably thinks about the church even while he's on vacation or traveling. I could sense his total commitment and dedication to serving Christ and the people of God.

It's like the scripture says that we have to be Christians in and out of season. I think he is a walking example of someone who likes being a priest, and is a priest in and out of season.

Closing

The original title of this book was: Ten Lessons I learn from Felino. Believe me when I say that I tried to come up with another lesson.

I decided to let time pass by and postpone the completion of this book with the hope that I could come up with just one more lesson, Since I couldn't come up with another lesson, I had to change the title to "9 lessons I learned from Fr. Felino."

Nevertheless, these 9 lessons are valuable for me, and I think may be helpful for those involved in parish ministry.

Admittedly, there are many pitfalls in parish ministry, and I myself have fallen through some of them. These 9 lessons, I think, are like flashlights that can help us to avoid some of those pitfalls.

I hope that you enjoy this book and share it with others. Please continue to pray for Fr. Felino and for myself, and the many priests, sisters, deacons, religious, and lay leaders. May we always be open to acquiring more priceless and valuable pearls for the sake of the Kingdom of God.

68670950R00022

Made in the USA
San Bernardino, CA
07 February 2018